LIVING ON THE OTHER SIDE OF BUT

JAN SCHWIEBERT

WESTBOW
PRESS®
A DIVISION OF THOMAS NELSON
& ZONDERVAN

This book is a work of non-fiction. Unless otherwise noted, the publisher makes no explicit guarantees as to the accuracy of the information contained in this book and in some cases, names of people and places have been altered to protect their privacy.

WestBow Press books may be ordered through booksellers or by contacting:

WestBow Press
A Division of Thomas Nelson & Zondervan
1663 Liberty Drive
Bloomington, IN 47403
www.westbowpress.com
1 (866) 928-1240

ISBN: 978-1-5127-9874-6 (sc)
ISBN: 978-1-5127-9876-0 (hc)
ISBN: 978-1-5127-9875-3 (e)

Library of Congress Control Number: 2017912523

Print information available on the last page.

WestBow Press rev. date: 9/20/2017

Dedicated to my precious Lord and Savior, who has captured me by his grace and revealed to me the joy and blessing of living on the other side of *but*.

CONTENTS

ACKNOWLEDGMENTS

As I have journeyed through this process of writing a book, I have realized more and more how important it is to have enthusiastic supporters and prayer partners to walk with me throughout the process. The book you have before you would have been impossible to write and bring to fruition had it not been for some very important people.

First of all is my husband, Loren, who has always supported and encouraged me, throughout the years, to be all God has created me to be and to do all God has called me to do. I can't imagine my life without him: the love of my life, my dearest friend, and my faithful companion. Thank you for being who you are.

I would also like to thank the women who have attended my classes at Grace Women. You have been such a blessing and have encouraged me in pursuing my dream of writing this book. I have loved and valued our times together.

I would also like to thank my sister, Jeanne Horn, for her proofreading, editing, and help in bringing this book through the birth pains into reality. I could never have done this without her. Even more than her editing skills, I want to thank her for just being herself, a loving sister who has made it very clear that there is nothing she wouldn't do or sacrifice to help me see my dreams come true.

I want to extend a special thanks to Reggie Adams and the staff at WestBow Press who patiently guided me through the whole process of having my book published and my dream become a reality.

INTRODUCTION

I'm sure we have all had some *aha* moments when something leaped off a page of scripture into our hearts. This happened, quite unexpectedly, one day when I was having my quiet time in the Word. How often had I ignored or passed over it? Such a little word but packed with so much power! It is the word *but*, which is the focus of this book.

Because God drew my attention to this little word, I have had the joy and adventure of opening God's Word in a fresh way—focusing on one word, *but*.

So often we live with the wrong focus, accepting beliefs about ourselves and/or our situations that are not true according to the Word of God. We live on a level far below what God intended for us because we are living on the wrong side of *but*.

This book is designed to give us hope that there is a better way; there is a way to live on the other side of *but*. We all have our stories, and I am sure that there are chapters in our stories that we wish weren't there and would not want anyone to read. *But* Jesus has come into our stories and covered those chapters with his forgiveness and love. He is inviting us now to live in the fullness of all He has provided—all that is possible on the other side of *but*.

I invite you to take this journey with me and experience life on the other side of *but*.

Chapter 1

Jesus Revealed on the Other Side of *But*

But we do see Jesus, who was made a little lower than the angels for a little while, now crowned with glory and honor because he suffered death, so that by the grace of God he might taste death for everyone.

—Hebrews 2:9 (NIV)

In Matthew 16:13–16, Jesus asked his disciples a very important question: "Who do men say that I am?" Some men thought Jesus was John the Baptist, Elijah, Jeremiah, or another of the prophets. They recognized that he spoke with authority and that many miracles occurred because of him, but they didn't perceive that he was much more.

Jesus asked them, "But who do you say that I am?"

Peter said, "You are the Christ." He and the other disciples had spent time with Jesus, heard his message, seen his heart, and witnessed his mighty miracles, through which they concluded that he was who he said he was.

The question is still important today. Who do men say Jesus is? The answers are just as confused today as they were in New Testament times. Many believe that Jesus was a good person and a good teacher. They accept that he did many good deeds and had many good things to say. However, they refuse to believe that he was the promised Savior and that he's God. There are people who reject many of his teachings as old-fashioned, irrelevant for today's society, and simply to be ignored. Some go so far as to deny his very existence. They claim the stories in the Bible are fantasy and have no foundation of truth.

There are also many of us who stand with Peter and say, "You are the Christ." At one time, we joined the Greek men who went to the disciples and asked to see Jesus. We knew that life had to have more meaning than what the world was offering. We knew, in our hearts, that we were in desperate shape. Some of us were in bondage, suffering from guilt and condemnation, or shamed due to situations we had created or had had thrust upon us; we always sought a different life but never quite experienced it. The future was without hope or purpose. But Jesus came into our lives, and a revelation of who he is and what he has done came too. Our first *but:* a revelation that brings hope and purpose.

> But we see Jesus, who was made a little lower than
> the angels for the suffering of death, crowned

with glory and honor; that he by the grace of God should taste death for every man. (Hebrews 2:9 KJV)

Discovering the Identity of Jesus

First let's look at a revelation of his identity. In John 1:1–4, we read that in the beginning was the Word, and the Word was made flesh and dwelt among us. So we know that Jesus has always been. These verses also reveal that nothing was created except through him. He was instrumental in the creation of the world. John leaves no doubt that Jesus is God in verse 1:18 "But the unique One, who is himself God, is near to the Father's heart. He has revealed God to us." A further declaration that Jesus is God is found in Romans 1:4: Jesus was "shown to be the Son of God when he was raised from the dead by the power of the Holy Spirit."

Why is it important to believe that Jesus is God? Why are Jesus's words so much more important than those of any other teacher? Many people have given their lives to a theory, an idea, or an ideology, but their lives ended in defeat and disillusionment. When we give our lives to Jesus and his teachings, we find life, hope, peace, and fulfillment. Why is this? Because Jesus is God! He "upholds all things by the word of his power," as it is written in Hebrews 1:3 (KJV). There is nothing too hard for him; in him are all potential and all possibilities. Why is this? Because Jesus is God! If we ignore scripture and refuse to face the truth of

Jesus's deity, we place ourselves outside the Word—a dangerous place to be.

Discovering Jesus's Mission

Next, let's look at his mission. If Jesus is God, and scripture tells us he is, then why would God come to earth as a baby, walk among sinful mankind, die the death of a criminal, and be raised from the dead? The answer is in that familiar scripture, John 3:16: "For this is how God loved the world: he gave his one and only Son, so that everyone who believes in him will not perish but have eternal life."

Just think! The Son of God became completely dependent on a young virgin named Mary and an earthly father, Joseph. He, the one without sin, lived among sinners. How could the holy, sinless one walk with the unholy, sinful ones? Love was the power behind that sacrifice. Then he suffered and died a horrendous death on the cross after being beaten and ridiculed by the very people he came to save. He gave himself up to death, as it is recorded in John 10:15, but on the third day, he rose and declared the victory over sin and death.

What an awesome story of redemption—the very reason Jesus came

- that we might have life and have it more abundantly (John 10:10)
- that we might be delivered out of the power of darkness (Colossians 1:13)
- that our sins might be forgiven (1 John 1:7)

- that we might be adopted into his family (Galatians 4:5)

How can we ever question his love for us?

Another mission that Jesus had was to reveal God the Father to us and bring us into a relationship with him. Jesus said that seeing him was seeing the Father and hearing him was hearing the Father. Jesus was doing his works in obedience to the Father who sent him.

In contrast to the false ideas and assumptions that we may have about God, Jesus clearly reveals to us that our Father God is a loving, healing, ever-present God who is *for* us. It is true that he does not tolerate sin, but that's why he sent Jesus to settle the sin issue. When we repent, he forgives. When we are in need, he meets that need with his love and compassion. We are told his mercies are new every morning.

If we have eyes to see and hearts to receive, reading the Old Testament does not contradict what Jesus revealed about God in the New Testament. Every time God spoke judgment to the people of Israel and Judah because they had gone after false gods, worshipped idols, and lived contrary to God's commands, he pleaded with them to repent and come back to him. Unconditional love never gives up on loved ones. If that can be true for us, how much more is it true of our good Father?

I remember when I settled God's goodness in my heart once and for all. My daughter called, crying, and told me that there had been a shooting where my granddaughter went to college.

I started crying and praying, "Lord, please don't let

Cassandra be hurt. You are a good God—" I stopped midsentence and declared, "Whether or not Cassandra got shot, you are a good God." His goodness is based on who he is and not on the circumstances that surround me. Once that was settled in my spirit, I stayed at peace until we heard the news that she was safe.

If all this is true, then there is only one appropriate response: Praise God for who he is and for what he has done and is doing.

As we think about all that the world worships and idolizes—success, materialism, power, sex—we are reminded of Psalm 20:7: "Some nations boast in their chariots and horses, but we boast in the name of the Lord our God."

We no longer sing the songs of our culture, praising things that have no eternal value. As the psalmist wrote in Psalm 40:3, "He has given me a new song to sing, a hymn of praise to our God."

We depend upon our God for all our needs. I am totally convinced that God can provide for us, his children, and move in ways that we can't understand or anticipate. This conviction comes from two sources—the Word and my story. It looked something like this: My husband lacked a job and had eight children to provide for, and we had a home that was anything less than desirable and very inexpensive, yet we could not pay the rent for six months. In all that time, we never lacked food on our table, clothes on our backs, or a roof over our heads. (The owner was so happy with the way we were taking care of his old homestead that he never pressed us for the rent—God's favor.)

Even though there may be times when our needs aren't met

the way we had anticipated, we can say, as in Psalm 28:7, "The Lord is my strength and shield. I trust him with all my heart. He helps me, and my heart is filled with joy. I burst out in songs of thanksgiving." This theme is found often in scripture, especially in the psalms.

Psalm 18:1–2 also declares the power and strength of the Lord working on our behalf: "I love you, Lord, you are my strength. The Lord is my rock ... in whom I find protection."

Responding to God's Revelation of Himself

In response to the revelation of our God, we are prompted to take two actions. The first one is found in Romans 12:1: "Give your bodies to God because of all he has done for you. Let them be a living and holy sacrifice—the kind he will find acceptable. This is truly the way to worship him." Powerful! Not only our words but our lives are to worship our God.

When we declare our great need for him and trust him with our lives, we worship him. When we surrender to his will and follow his path for our lives, we worship him. When we are overwhelmed with all he has given us in this life and all the ways we have been so richly blessed, we worship him. When our focus is on him instead of ourselves or our circumstances, we worship him. When we reach out to others with the love of Christ, we worship him. Get the picture? When we consider all God has done and is doing for us, our hearts compel us to live lives that are pleasing to our Almighty God.

One other response is found in Revelation 4:8—a response coming from our hearts, acknowledging the greatness and the holiness of our God: "Holy, holy, holy is the Lord God, the Almighty—the one who always was, who is, and who is still to come."

No matter how much is revealed to us about our God, we will never plumb the depths of who he is. It makes me think of experiencing an ocean. Our experience begins by viewing the surface of the water. Next we might decide to take a swim. Our adventure continues when we put on scuba gear and go deeper into the ocean. If, by some chance, we are invited onto a submarine, we could go even deeper into the ocean. No matter how deep we go, no matter how much we see, there is more. What beauty awaits us as we go deeper into the ocean? It was there all the time, but we had yet to experience it.

Jesus, revealed on the other side of *but,* brings us the revelation that he is holy, loving, compassionate, kind, good, gentle, faithful, patient, and long-suffering. He is life; he is truth; he alone is the way to God and to our eternal destiny in heaven. He is our Savior, our healer, the victorious one, ruling in righteousness—the One who upholds all creation by the word of his power. He is clothed in splendor, clothed in glory, and seated in majesty. Yes, we could go on, but I think you have the picture. But we see Jesus! Hallelujah!

Thoughts to Ponder

1. How would you answer the questions Jesus asked his disciple: "Who do men say that I am?" and "Who do you say that I am?"

2. Why are our beliefs about God important?

3. Think of a time when God revealed himself to you in a special way. How has that impacted your life?

Chapter 2

Impossibilities Made Possible on the Other Side of *But*

Jesus looked at them intently and said, "Humanly speaking, it is impossible. But not with God. Everything is possible with God."

—Mark 10:27

H ave you ever faced a task, an assignment, or a challenge that you said was impossible? No matter what the seemingly impossible challenge might be, the good news is that the impossible becomes possible with God. Nothing catches God by surprise. Nothing that has happened in our lives is so horrendous that God throws up his hands and says, "I wasn't expecting that. I'm not sure how to handle this crisis." God is always in control. He is all-powerful, and nothing is too hard for him. Scripture tells us that, humanly speaking, something may be impossible, but not with God. All things are possible with God, as we read in Matthew 19:26 and Mark 10:27.

The power for the miraculous is in the Word of God, in the power of the name of Jesus, and in the working of the Holy Spirit. The first place to witness the impossible becoming possible is in the Word.

Witnessing the Miraculous Power of God in Scripture

In the Old Testament, we read of many instances where God revealed his miraculous working power when, in the natural world, there was no way for deliverance. One powerful example, of course, is when Moses and the children of Israel were fleeing Egypt (Ex.14:13-31). They came to an impossibility. There was a sea before them, mountains on either side of them, and the Egyptian army in chariots behind them. They were doomed, but God came to their rescue. He sent a strong wind to divide the waters so the children of Israel could cross over to the other side. When the Egyptians in their chariots tried to follow, he closed the water, and the army of Egypt was destroyed. An impossibility became possible.

Another powerful Old Testament account of an impossibility becoming possible is the story of the three Hebrew men in the fiery furnace. When they refused to bow to the statue of King Nebuchadnezzar, they were thrown into a fiery furnace. It was so hot, in fact, that the soldiers throwing them into the furnace were killed by the fire. After many minutes, it became clear that they were not going to burn; in fact, a fourth presence had joined them. When they were removed from the furnace, there was no trace of the fire on their bodies, not even a smell of smoke. How did it happen? Such an outcome is impossible with men but possible with God.

Then there is the account of Joshua marching for seven days around the city of Jericho (Joshua 6). On the seventh day, the children of Israel walked around the city seven times and then blew the trumpets and shouted. When they did, the walls of the city fell, and they were able to enter the city and experience a great victory. Another impossibility? But not with God!

There are so many Old Testament stories that we could share, but now we are going to look to the New Testament for some examples.

The first one that comes to mind is the birth of Jesus—truly a miracle—an impossibility made possible. A seed, the very Son of God, was planted in the womb of a virgin. The Son of God entered humanity as a helpless baby. This impossibility makes all that follows possible.

In Luke 9:10–17, we read that Jesus faced a hungry multitude of over five thousand people in a place where there was nothing for them to eat. Instead of sending them away hungry, Jesus took five loaves and two fish given by a small boy, prayed over them, and had the disciples feed the multitude. When everyone was fed, there were still twelve baskets of food left to be gathered by the disciples. An impossible task was made possible by the miracle-working power of the Savior.

From Acts 10:38, we learn that Jesus went around doing

good and healing all who were oppressed by the devil. One account of healing is found in Mark 5:25–34, in which we read that a woman who had an issue of blood for twelve years said that if she could just touch the hem of his garment, she would be healed. She pressed through the crowd to get to Jesus and touched the hem of his garment, and immediately the bleeding stopped. Jesus knew that healing had flowed from him and called out for the one who had touched him. When she came forward, he said that her faith had healed her. An illness that the doctors had been unable to treat successfully for twelve years, a seeming impossibility, was healed in a moment when she touched Jesus in faith.

Talk about an impossibility! There are three accounts of Jesus raising the dead.

Jairus, a leader in a local synagogue, pleaded with Jesus to come and heal his daughter. When they arrived at his house, they met mourners who said that his daughter had died. Jesus sent everyone but the parents, Peter, James, and John from her room and then told her, "Little girl, get up." She was brought back to life by the power of his word. Impossible, one might say, but it was made possible by the command of Jesus. (See Mark 5.)

In John 11 we read the account of the miraculous raising of Lazarus. He had been dead four days by the time Jesus arrived at his home. His sisters cried to Jesus that if only he had come sooner, he could have healed their brother. It was then that Jesus declared, "I am the resurrection and the life." He proceeded to the tomb where Lazarus was buried, ordered the stone to be rolled away, and ordered Lazarus to come out of the grave, and

Lazarus did. Dead four days, he was alive again! His return to life was an impossibility but possible because Jesus has power over death and the grave.

The third account is found in Luke 7:11–15. When Jesus and his disciples came into the city of Nain, he encountered a funeral procession. A widow had lost her only son, and they were on their way to bury him. Jesus interrupted their plans in a powerful way. He stopped the procession and ordered the boy to get up. The dead boy got up, and Jesus gave him back to his mother. Life conquered death—impossible but possible when Jesus intervenes.

These accounts demonstrate that Jesus has victory over the plans of the enemy. Those plans are specified in John 10:10: "The thief's purpose is to steal and kill and destroy. My purpose is to give them a rich and satisfying life."

What a joy it is to know that, by the power of the Holy Spirit, impossibilities are still made possible. It began on the day of Pentecost when the Holy Spirit was poured out on the 120 believers in the upper room. Evidence of the miraculous is recorded in Acts. For example, in Acts 3:1–10, when Peter and John were going to the temple, a man who had been born crippled cried out to them for a handout.

Peter told him, "I don't have any silver or gold for you. But I'll give you what I have. In the name of Jesus Christ of Nazareth, get up and walk." We are told that he got up immediately— walking, leaping, and praising God. How does a man who was born a cripple, a man never able to walk, immediately get up and not only walk but dance and jump? It would be impossible for man, but it is made possible by the power of the Holy Spirit and the name of Jesus.

Contrary to some teaching that all miracles ended at the death of the disciples, that we can no longer expect the impossible to become possible, the good news is that God is still God. He is the same yesterday, today, and forever; he is still very much involved in the affairs of mankind. He has never lost his power or his will to move powerfully in the lives of people who call on him in faith. Impossibilities are still becoming possible.

Witnessing the Miraculous Power of God Today

The miracle of the new birth is the greatest impossibility that became possible because of the cross. There is no way we could make ourselves right with God. We were spiritually dead even as Lazarus was physically dead. Life came from God to produce life in us. We come into a relationship with Jesus because of what he did. It was impossible for us to be good enough or do enough to earn salvation. It is also impossible for us to live a life pleasing to God on our own. In John 15:15, Jesus said that he is the vine, and we are the branches. Apart from him, we can do nothing. But as his children, we aren't alone and can be, as the disciples were, messengers of hope and conduits for the miraculous. We can be participants and witnesses to impossibilities still being made possible.

Here are some examples.

I saw a woman who had a heart murmur instantly healed as a result of prayer, a little girl with severe asthma set free, legs lengthened, an addiction overcome, food provided when the cupboards were almost empty, money provided when there was no job to provide income, and depression lifted—all made possible by the power of the Holy Spirit. God will provide a supernatural peace in the midst of great challenges, unspeakable joy in the midst of great tragedy, and love and forgiveness in a season of betrayal and hurt. When I declare that something is impossible for me to do or control, I am correct. I can't but God can. That is the truth I can hold on to when I am in a time of crisis.

I want to share with you one final testimony to declare that the miraculous healing power of God is still working in the lives of people. (This is something I witnessed, so I know it is true.) A pastor's wife shared with a group of us the following miracle. As a young teenager, she went to church camp. While she was there, she requested prayer for her blind eye, which had been replaced with a glass one. God heard and answered her prayer. She could then see out of that eye. She demonstrated to us: With her good eye covered, she could read with or without the glass eye in its socket. Truly a miracle only God could perform!

May we take to heart and be encouraged by the words of Jesus in Mark 10:27 (NIV): "Jesus looked at them and said, 'With men this is impossible, but not with God; all things are possible with God.'"

Thoughts to Ponder

1. Think of a time you faced an impossible situation. How did God show you that all things are possible in him?

2. What is your favorite biblical account of an impossibility becoming possible because God showed up? How does that story affect the way you deal with the impossibilities of your life?

3. What is the greatest miracle you have either heard of or experienced? What impact has it had on how you see God?

CHAPTER 3

Love and Acceptance Discovered on the Other Side of *But*

But God showed his great love for us by sending
Christ to die for us while we were still sinners.

—Romans 5:8

T he word *love* is used loosely in our culture. We love a certain food, a sports team, a special restaurant, a famous movie, and so on. Then there is the love of a parent for a child, a child for a parent, a love of siblings, of friends, of a spouse. The only problem with this love is that it is often conditional, and conditional love is tied to what we do or don't do. When we have failed to meet someone's expectations, we are often rejected or challenged to earn that person's love and acceptance again. This, of course, is tied to the matter of forgiveness. The inability to be forgiven reveals a conditional love offered by the one who refused to extend forgiveness or love.

God gave me a powerful illustration of his unconditional love when we brought two foster girls into our home. They were rebellious, defiant, and determined not to respond positively to our family. God gave me such a love for them. No matter how they treated us or what they said, no matter if they lied, stole, or defied us, I just loved them. God revealed to me what unconditional love looks like—the kind of love he has for us. It is not based on how the person being loved performs or if that person deserves love; it is an expression of the heart from the one doing the loving.

Discovering God's Love

The good news is that God's love is unconditional. It doesn't depend on how we perform. It is rooted in who God is: He is love. This became so clear to me in a very personal way one day when I was ironing and listening to Joy Dawson teaching on a cassette tape. (Remember those?) This wasn't her topic, but what she said triggered this revelation: God loves me because he is love. I can't do anything to make him love me more or less. His love is not based on my performance but on who he is. What a liberating truth! From Genesis to Revelation, we receive a revelation of the God who loves and is, in fact, love.

In the Old Testament, we find God's own words concerning his faithfulness and steadfast love. He says in Isaiah 54:10, "For the mountains may move and the hills disappear, but even then my faithful love for you will remain." Circumstances may change, but God's love will never change. It can't. That would be contrary to his very nature.

In Jeremiah 9:24 we read, "But those who wish to boast should boast in this alone; that they truly know me and understand that I am the Lord who demonstrates unfailing love and who brings justice and righteousness to the earth." It seems quite remarkable that God Almighty delights in us and delights in proving his love for us.

In the Book of Psalms, we find many references to God's unfailing love that should give each of us reason to feel secure in the truth that God loves us individually. What a blessing to be able to declare with David in Psalm 36:7, "How precious is your unfailing love, O God! All humanity finds shelter in the shadow of your wings." This statement is an acknowledgment that we are safe in his love.

In Psalm 42:8, we also read, "But each day the Lord pours his unfailing love upon me."

In Psalm 63:3, we acknowledge the truth and respond to God in praise that "your unfailing love is better than life itself, how I praise you."

These psalms and many others assure us that because of his love, we are safe; no matter what our circumstances may look like, we can trust in a God who never changes, who tenderly loves and cares for us under the shadow of his wings.

Our recognition of and response to this love is found in Psalm 136; in twenty-six verses, the psalmist tells us to give thanks and ends each verse with the refrain, "His faithful love endures forever." God's deeds in the Old Testament proved his love and faithfulness to his people. Those deeds demonstrating his might and power deserve to be recognized for what they were—a demonstration of his faithful love.

One final verse from the Old Testament that I want to emphasize is Micah 7:18—"Where is another God like you, who pardons the guilt of the remnant, overlooking the sins of his special people. You will not stay angry with your people forever, because you delight in showing unfailing love."

Just meditate on that last phrase for a moment. God delights in showing unfailing love; it gives him pleasure to love us.

This brings us to a key verse for this chapter, Romans 5:8: "But God demonstrates his own love for us in this: while we were yet sinners, Christ died for us." To underscore this truth, we are going to look at God's love in three ways: his love identified, his love demonstrated, and his love embraced. But first I want to share a story of a mother hen and her chicks that was told by Dr. Larry Petton.

> It was a hot day in the dry Old West. As the railroad came roaring down the tracks, sparks were flying because of the hot temperatures. When the sparks flew, often they would begin a fire that would destroy ranches, homes, and livestock. One particular day there was a fire that spread from a railroad train in West Texas and did major damage. As the old farmer who owned

the property walked through the ashes of his home and ranch, he saw an old hen lying on the ground, burned to death. Her wings were spread open. In his anger, he kicked the old hen. To his surprise, several baby chicks ran out from under her burned wings. When the fire had come, the hen had draped herself over her little ones and taken the fire to save their lives.

That is a picture of the gospel. That is an illustration of the great love of our Savior. We have a Savior who did exactly that for us. When the fire of God's holy wrath should have consumed us, Christ spread out his arms on the cross and covered us in his blood. That sacrifice makes it possible for us to be protected and safe in the loving arms of our God—experiencing love on the other side of *but*.

God's love is identified in many New Testament passages, including Ephesians 3:16: "And may you have the power to understand as all God's people should, how wide, how long, how high, and how deep his love is." In other words, there is no limit to God's love.

God's love is also proclaimed in John 1:14 and 1:17: "So the word became human and made his home among us. He was full of unfailing love and faithfulness ... For the law was given through Moses, but God's unfailing love and faithfulness came through Jesus Christ." The very entrance into humanity of Jesus, the Son of God, is a powerful witness of the love and faithfulness of God Almighty.

And because words are not enough, he gave and is still giving demonstrations of that love. The familiar passage, John 3:16, reads, "God so loved the world that he sent his one and only son."

In Ephesians 1:4, we read, "But God is so rich in mercy and he loved us so much, that even though we were dead because of our sins, he gave us life when he raised Christ Jesus from the dead."

This outrageous love is confirmed in Titus 3:4–5: "But when God our Savior revealed his kindness and love, he saved us, not because of the righteous things we had done, but because of his mercy." Talk about unconditional love!

He loves us so much, in fact, that we are called his children in 1 John 3:1. That he would identify with us, claim us as his own, and love us as a father loves his child is overwhelming. I know myself; he knows me more and still loves me. What a truth to embrace!

The truth of God's love and faithfulness is revealed many other places in scripture as well. We have looked at some of these verses that share the identification and the demonstration of God's love. When we meditate on the awesome love of God that he so powerfully reveals and demonstrates to us, the only proper response is to love him with all our hearts, our souls, our minds, and our strength and to live lives of worship and praise to the One of whom Romans 5:8 declares: "But God showed his great love for us by sending Christ to die for us while we were still sinners."

Embracing God's Love

We need to embrace what God so freely gives instead of dwelling on all the reasons God couldn't love us. Instead of looking at all the challenges in our world and concluding that God isn't love and doesn't care, we need to refuse the lies of the devil—and they are lies—and receive the Word of God. From cover to cover, it says just the opposite. God *is* love; therefore, he loves. We can have the assurance of God's love as stated in Romans 5:5: "And this hope will not disappoint. For we know how dearly God loves us, because he has given us the Holy Spirit to fill our hearts with his love."

Then, too, we can say what Paul wrote in Romans 8:38–39: "I am convinced that nothing can ever separate us from God's love … indeed, nothing in all creation will ever be able to separate us from the love of God that is revealed in Christ Jesus our Lord."

A precious picture of assurance is found in Jude 1:21: "And await the mercy of our Lord, Jesus Christ, who will bring you eternal life. In this way, you will keep yourselves safe in God's love." Can't you just see yourself being held lovingly and securely in the arms of our Lord and cradled in his love?

The first illustration that comes to my mind is Boots, my little dog. Boots will climb up onto the chair with me and just cuddle with me. He doesn't want anything; he just wants to be close to me. That's how I see myself: cuddled up with my precious Lord, cradled in his love.

The other illustration is a picture I have of a hand, and

resting in that hand is a bird. To me, it is a picture of God holding me in his loving hand, where I am safe, protected, and tended.

It is vital that we are convinced that God is love and that he loves us unconditionally. It breaks the bondage of performance and perfectionism. It breaks the strongholds of rejection and insecurities. If I truly believe I am loved unconditionally by God Almighty, it takes away any fear in my relationship with him—wondering if I'm good enough, if my shame is too great, if my deficiencies outnumber my abilities.

The devil has so many ways to lie to us and lay before us all our imperfections and all our actions that weren't righteous. But God's love revealed through Jesus breaks through all those lies and all those barriers. When believed, it sets us free to love and be loved, to experience all God has for us and to be all God created us to be. "God so loved the world ..." includes you! Loved and cherished by a mighty God, safe in his loving care, you may embrace his love and walk in the freedom of that love. Remember you are living on the other side of *but*, where our loving God lavishes love and acceptance upon us.

Thoughts to Ponder

1. What are some experiences that keep people from believing that God's love is unconditional?

2. Think of a time when you came face to face with the reality of God's love for you. How has that encounter affected your relationship with him?

3. What does it mean to "walk in the freedom of his love," as stated at the end of this chapter?

CHAPTER 4

New Life Experienced on the Other Side of *But*

For the wages of sin is death, but the free gift of
God is eternal life through Christ Jesus our Lord.

—Romans 6:23

In the key verse for this chapter, Romans 6:23, we read, "The wages of sin is death, the gift of God is eternal life in Christ our Lord." Note the powerful contrast: Wages are payments a person earns; a person receives gifts without doing anything to earn them. If someone works a forty-hour week in a job that pays ten dollars per hour, he or she can expect to be paid $400.00 at the end of that week. A salary is rightfully earned. But if a person who cannot work is given $400.00, that person has received a blessing, a gift that has not been earned. If we walk in sin and disobedience, our paycheck is death. However, if we choose by the Spirit to receive the gift of eternal life through Jesus, we receive life, a gift that we did not earn. What a powerful *but*.

In the garden of Eden, God told Adam and Eve that everything there, with one exception, was for their enjoyment; however, they were not to eat the fruit of the tree of the knowledge of good and evil. If they disobeyed, they would die. They did disobey; they ate the fruit. And they got their paycheck—death, separation from God, and removal from the garden. Their bodies would eventually die, but their spirits died immediately, as it is written in Genesis 3.

Sin had now entered the world and manifested through their two sons. Cain became jealous of his brother Abel because God accepted Abel's sacrifice but not his. God warned Cain that "sin is crouching at your door." Cain ignored the warning and killed Abel. He received his paycheck: He was forced to become a homeless wanderer (Genesis 4:1–19). The story of Cain was written as an example for us. Sin always has a paycheck.

Receiving Sin's Paycheck

Before going any further, it might be a good idea to define sin. First John 3:4 defines sin in this way: "Everyone who sins is breaking God's law, for all sin is contrary to the law of God." One translation uses *lawlessness* to define sin. According to the Word, there is pleasure in sin for a moment. But it also tells us that with the pleasure comes a paycheck: bondages, addictions, alienation, shame, guilt, condemnation, rejection, and death.

This scenario is described vividly for us in Galatians 6:8: "Those who live only to satisfy their own sinful nature will harvest decay and death from that sinful nature, but those who live to please the Spirit will harvest everlasting life from the Spirit." We are encouraged, therefore, by its message.

> Put to death the sinful earthly things lurking with
> you. Have nothing to do with sexual immorality,
> impurity, lust, and evil desires. Don't be greedy,
> for a greedy person is an idolater, worshiping the
> things of this world. Because of these sins, the
> anger of God is coming. (Colossians 3:5–6)

We have to make a choice: Put those things to death. The power to live up to that choice comes from the Holy Spirit, who resides in every believer. People have the misconception that they can live any way they choose and have no consequences. They don't realize that the cost of that decision is eternal death—a paycheck no one would really want.

The good news is that we can live on the other side of this *but* and walk in the blessings of our gift instead of the paycheck of our sin. The bridge is found in passages such as 1 Corinthians 6:9–11. First it lists many sins and says that those practicing them cannot inherit eternal life. Happily for us, it doesn't stop there. Instead, here comes the *but*: "Some of you were once like that but you were cleansed, you were made holy, you were made right with God by calling on the name of the Lord Jesus Christ and by the Spirit of our God." Paul states the case further in Romans.

> Therefore, dear brothers and sisters, you have no obligation to do what your sinful nature urges you to do. For if you live by its dictates, you will die. But if through the power of the Spirit you put to death the deeds of your sinful nature, you will live. (Romans 8:12–13)

The provision to make the right choice—in itself is a gift—comes from God by the power of the Spirit. It is up to us to accept the gift he offers.

Receiving the Gift God Offers

What does this gift look like, one might wonder? The gift, pure and simple, is God himself, resident in our lives with his eternal life. We are free from the power of sin to inflict a heavy paycheck when we accept his gift of eternal life—a life lived in the presence and power of our living God, a life that produces fruits. These fruits are love, joy, peace, patience, kindness, goodness, faithfulness, gentleness, and self-control (Galatians 5:22–23). Notice that these fruits are the *results* of the gift of eternal life, not a *prerequisite* for receiving eternal life. We did nothing to earn this new life, but we can choose to live in the newness of this life because of the power of God's life within us or continue with the false belief that somehow we need to be good enough or do enough to earn it. When we fall back into that way of thinking, we are back to the concept that eternal life is earned.

How many people when asked if they will go to heaven when they die respond with a, "Yes," or "I hope so,"? When asked what they base their hope on, their response is, "Well, I've lived a pretty good life, tried to be honest, and done my part."

All these are reasons based on their performance. The problem is that they will never be good enough. The Bible says that if we sin in even one of the commandments, we have sinned against all (James 2:10). The other problem is that they are comparing their lives with people who have done some awful deeds instead of comparing their lives with a holy God. When we do that, we don't come out looking that great, realizing that if we have to be holy as God is holy, we will never succeed. That's why salvation, eternal life, is a gift. We can't earn it; we can only receive what God has made available to us.

I read a passage in Larry Osborne's *Accidental Pharisee.*

> Jesus played the Pharisee card in his famous Sermon on the Mount. To illustrate the impossibility of earning our way into heaven, he pointed to a series of well-known moral standards from the law of Moses. Using the words "you have heard … but I tell you … he took six commands they thought they could keep and replaced each one with a standard they could never achieve. Don't commit murder became don't even be angry with your brother … or don't commit adultery

turned into a prohibition of lustful thoughts and wandering eyes.[1]

Jesus wanted us to understand that it is impossible to stand before a holy God, justified by our own good deeds and righteousness.

When we read that the wages of sin is death, we should raise our hands in despair, for we are all sinners doomed to spend eternity in hell: That's our paycheck. But it doesn't have to be. You see, Jesus invites us to live on the other side of the *but*. At an invitation, a response is always required—a RSVP, if you will. If we say *yes*, we will live with an eternal perspective and an eternal destiny. The decision is ours. If you have never said *yes* to Jesus's invitation, I would invite you to stop reading right now, bow your heart humbly before the Lord, confess your sin and disobedience by trying to live your life without him, and invite him to come in and be the Lord of your life. That's receiving the gift freely offered and earned for you on the cross.

In response to this gift, either for the first time or in recognition that such a gift has been offered and received at some juncture of your life, there are a few things that we are encouraged to do—not to earn our salvation but in response to our salvation.

"Just think how much more the blood of Christ will purify our consciences from sinful deeds so that we can worship the living God," we read in Hebrews 9:14. The realization that we no longer have to carry the burden of our sins or be buried in

---

[1] Larry Osborne. *Accidental Pharisees.* (Grand Rapids: MI: Zondervan, 2012.)

guilt and condemnation because of what Jesus has done for us should inspire us to worship our holy and loving God.

First Peter 2:5 tells us that "through the mediation of Jesus Christ, you offer spiritual sacrifices that please God." These sacrifices are, according to Romans 12:1, our bodies presented to God "as a living and holy sacrifice—the kind he will find acceptable." This is truly the way to worship him.

It cannot be stressed enough that our worship, appreciation, and gratitude flow from our relationship with our God because of the gift given and received on the merit of his sacrifice at the cross and not through any merit found in us. If we had to earn eternal life, it would no longer be a gift. I realize this point is repeated several times in this chapter, but because we are so prone to performance for acceptance, it really can't be overstated.

When we understand and receive the gift, we will experience the joy, peace, and freedom that come with it. I know many of you reading this book have had that experience. I know I have, and my prayer is that those of you who had not known such joy and peace have now discovered the secret of the gift and received it: new life in Jesus.

I want to end this chapter with a story about a priceless pearl.

There was a man who had a great burden for the people of India, so he set out to share the gospel with them in hopes that many would be saved. Over time, he made friends with a man called Raoul. He tried repeatedly to witness to Raoul, sharing the gospel and giving the good news of salvation through the blood of Jesus. Raoul just couldn't grasp that it would be that easy; just ask Jesus into his heart and all his sins could be forgiven. Surely, there was some sacrifice he would have to make, something he would have to do for his salvation, to take away his sin.

One day, Raoul came to the missionary and told him he was planning to crawl to New Delhi to earn favor with his god. The missionary tried to discourage him, telling him how hard it would be, how painful it would become, but Raoul said he had to do it to please his god.

The day came when Raoul was to set out on his pilgrimage. He came to the missionary carrying a box which he presented to the missionary. "I want you to have this because you have been my friend and have been so kind to me."

When the missionary opened the box, there was a beautiful pearl. The missionary said, "I cannot take this; it is too valuable." Raoul kept insisting that he wanted him to have it. The missionary said, "Raoul, how much money do you want for this?"

Raoul replied, "No, it is free for you."

The missionary said, "I have friends in the States that might be able to collect an offering so that I can give you more money for this beautiful pearl."

But grieving, Raoul replied, "You don't understand. My son was a sea diver, and he went deep into the water to find this pearl. It cost him his life, so it is very precious to me, and I want to give it to you."

The missionary responded, "Raoul, that's what God did for you. Jesus came and gave his life and wants to present this gift of salvation to you—a gift too precious, too valuable for you to earn it; it is a gift."

Raoul finally saw the truth and was saved.[2]

And that, I would add, is what God has done for you as well.

---

[2] Alice Gray (comp.). "The Matchless Pearl." *Stories for a Faithful Heart.* (Sisters, OR: Multnomah, 2000).

Thoughts to Ponder

1. How do you determine if your relationship with God is based more on grace or on works?

2. What would you say to someone who hoped for heaven because he or she lived a good life?

3. How does one break free from a performance-based relationship with Jesus?

CHAPTER 5

Victorious Living Realized
on the Other Side of *But*

In the same way, count yourselves dead to sin but
alive to God in Christ Jesus.

—Romans 6:11 (NIV)

Who sets out to be a loser? Everyone has that desire to be a winner, to succeed in anything they try, to be the best at anything they do.

We see this in sports. When men and women train for the Olympics, their eyes are on winning the gold. They do not put in hours of conditioning and training for the Olympics to lose. They are there to win. Managers of professional baseball, basketball, or football teams bargain for the players they feel will be assets to their teams and help them win the games. If they are on a losing streak, they evaluate the games and players to determine if someone needs to be traded or a coach needs to be replaced because the goal is to manage a champion team.

We see this in large corporations. On their management teams are men and women they feel will cause the corporation to prosper and be the best in its field. They are always looking for ways to be more successful.

In school, the good students always strive to get As, to excel in their studies, and to come out ahead of the others. When playing and competing, children have one goal, and that is to win. We think it unnatural if someone is not competitive, not working to take home the trophy or the top prize, not longing for the recognition of being the best in some endeavor. (Our culture, I might add, is fighting hard to remove a competitive spirit from games and grades so that no boy or girl feels badly about performance.) But even in scripture, we are told that the purpose of training is to win. In 1 Corinthians 9:24, we read, "Don't you realize that in a race everyone runs, but only one person gets the prize? So, run to win!"

Making a Choice

When anyone who plays to win loses, it is devastating or, at the least, very disappointing. But even more devastating are those who are spiritual losers—men and women who are in bondage to sin and can't seem to rise above the sin to a place of victory. No matter how much they try to put their failures in the past, not to be repeated, the defeat lingers and sometimes intensifies. Just as muscles become stronger as they are met with resistance, so sin becomes stronger as it is met with resistance in one's own strength. In that scenario, the conclusion becomes, "I'm a loser. I will never get free from the sins of my past or the failures and bondages that still enslave me." And that is true—if there weren't a *but*.

In 1 Corinthians 9:25, we have the goal of victory put in its proper place: "All athletes are disciplined in their training. They do it to win a prize that will fade away. But we do it for an eternal prize."

Again we see that God's plans are bigger and better. It is always greater to live on the other side of *but*. The one brings victory for a season, and then it's gone. The other brings victory for eternity, which never ends.

In 2 Timothy 2:5, we read that "athletes cannot win the prize unless they follow the rules." When looking at this race of life, we need to know what the rules are—how is it possible to live on the right side of *but*?

It is found in Romans 6:11, the key verse: "In the same way, count yourselves dead to sin but alive to God in Christ Jesus." I remember the first time I heard a teaching on this scripture. I was greatly challenged by the revelation that a dead man has no rights. I am no longer in charge of my life; God is. It is no longer all about me, what I want, or what I need. Now when I am tempted to demand my rights, I remind myself that the old man is dead and has no rights.

Living in Victory

There are two aspects of experiencing the life Jesus has for us, the one he paid so dearly for us to receive.

The first is that we consider ourselves dead to sin. We have a powerful example of one who did just that, Joseph. He was sold into slavery by his brothers, but he did not let bitterness overcome him or dictate how he would live. As a slave, he showed himself to be honorable and gained favor with Potiphar. A temptation to sin came in the person of Potiphar's wife. She tried to seduce him, but he continued to say *no* to her. As told in Genesis 39:9 (KJV), Joseph's reason was, "How can I do this great wickedness and sin against God?" His relationship with God was more important to him than the pleasure of sin.

On the other side, as recorded in 2 Samuel 11–12, King David gave in to temptation and allowed the pleasure of sin, adultery, to win out. Sin has results too. But fortunately for David and for us, it doesn't have to define us or defeat us. David repented, as related in Psalm 51, and was back in a relationship with his God—even described by God as a "man after his own heart" in Acts 13:22. Through the power of forgiveness and restoration, David became dead to sin but alive in God. Did David have the same power to resist the temptation that Joseph did? Of course the answer is *yes,* because they both had a relationship with God that told them what was right and what was wrong and the power to make the right choice.

Most excitingly, we not only have a relationship with God that tells us what is right and wrong; we have the power of the

Holy Spirit to draw on to make the right choices. Romans states this powerfully in many verses. Let's look at a few of them.

> But now you are free from the power of sin and have become slaves of God. Now you do those things that lead to holiness and result in eternal life. (Romans 6:21)

> You have no obligation to do what your sinful nature urges you to do. For if you live by its dictates you will die. But if through the power of the Spirit you put to death the deeds of your sinful nature, you will live. (Romans 8:12–13)

We make a choice; the Holy Spirit empowers us to gain the victory over the temptation.

> You were dead because of your sins and because your sinful nature was not yet cut away. Then God made you alive with Christ, for he forgave all our sins. (Colossians 2:13)

First Peter 2:24 declares, "He personally carried our sins in his body on the cross so that we can be dead to sin and live for what is right."

Now we come to the other point in the verse: we are "alive to God in Christ Jesus." Because we are flesh and blood and are functioning with the everyday things in our lives, we don't realize that without Christ, we are dead people walking. This is a more devastating death than taking our last breaths and being declared officially, physically dead. This is an eternal death, a separation from God forever—one that never ends.

That may not mean much for an unbeliever who has had no interest in God or one who has rebelled against him. However, we know that God is God. "He upholds all things by the word of his power," as we read in Hebrews 1:3. If he were not raining on the just and the unjust, if he were not present in the affairs of man, the world would be in total darkness. Just look at the depravity in a person or a country where there is no light, honor, truth, integrity, or righteousness. So when we are told that "he made us alive with Christ," we should sit up and take notice and then spend the rest of our lives in worship and surrender to the One who brought us life.

When we said *yes* to Jesus, we were embracing life itself. Colossians 3:3 tells us that "you died to this life, and your real life is hidden with Christ in God." What an exchange—spiritual death for everlasting life in Christ. Only a God who loves us would come up with such a plan! God's plan is one that I can't comprehend with my mind, but I wholly embrace that plan with my heart. "For God presented Jesus as the sacrifice for sin. People are made right with God when they believe that Jesus sacrificed his life, shedding his blood," as it is written in Romans 3:25, and they make the great exchange.

We can shout in agreement with 2 Corinthians 5:17 that we are "new creations in Christ Jesus" and that "the old life is gone; a new life has begun." How does that happen? The great exchange is at work.

As if it couldn't get any better, Galatians 4:5 reveals to us that "God sent him [Jesus] to buy freedom for us who were slaves to the law, so that he could adopt us as his very own children." We are alive in Christ, and we are his, a part of his family forever because of the life of Jesus within us. What an awesome God and plan!

Sharing a Personal Testimony

Here is the scenario that played out: my testimony. I was living a life driven by guilt and condemnation. The only way I felt I could get approval was by being perfect. Because I found it impossible to live by the standard I had set for myself, my feelings of guilt and condemnation deepened. My sense of rejection intensified. To put it plainly, I was miserable, desperate for unconditional love and acceptance. But I was introduced to a precious Savior who loves me and gave his life for me so that I could be set free from the bondages that held me. Into my heart and life came Jesus. The light dispelled the darkness, and I was set free from the bondages of guilt and condemnation. I would like to say I immediately experienced total freedom and life in every area; however, that was not my experience. Over the years, as the revelation of who Jesus is in me and who I am in him has become clearer, the freedom, the life that I longed for, has become more real. It was always there through the love of Jesus and the power of the cross, but I had to embrace it and learn to walk in it.

In John 1 we read that the light expelled the darkness. If you were in a room that was totally dark and lit a match, the light from that match would consume the darkness around it. The dark would not extinguish that light. So it is with our lives when Jesus, by the Holy Spirit, resides in our lives; his light begins to consume the darkness. Things are exposed, brought into the light, by the life of the One who now lives in us. As the light and life of his presence continue to reveal and heal, we begin to experience the freedom and life for which we yearned. He has promised in John 10:10 that he has come to bring us abundant, overflowing life. That is his promise; may we embrace his provision for that to happen and experience the life it cost him so much to provide. May we do as Romans 6:11 instructs us to do: count ourselves dead to sin but alive to God in Christ Jesus.

Thoughts to Ponder

1. Express in your own words the "great exchange."

2. How can someone bound in sin or addictions break free and stay free?

3. How does (or would) your life look different if you are or were living victoriously on the other side of *but*?

CHAPTER 6

New Identity Embraced on the Other Side of *But*

My old self has been crucified with Christ. It is no
longer I who live, but Christ lives in me. So I live
in this earthly body by trusting in the Son of God,
who loved me and gave himself for me.

—Galatians 2:20

We had the opportunity to have several foster children in
our home. One of the real heartbreakers was a young
girl named Lucy. She came from a very dysfunctional family
and was one of five siblings. When she started school, she was
thriving. When she entered the fourth grade, the teacher labeled
her: "Oh, she's one of those kids." With that expectation from
her teacher, she began to fail classes and to assume the label the

school put on her: a loser. That's how she ended up in our home. She then saw herself through the eyes of those who had rejected her because of her last name, not because of who she was and her potential. We are so often identified and labeled according to our family ties, our appearance, or what we have done rather than who we are as individuals.

The good news is that those who have come into a relationship with the Lord Jesus have a new identity and new label. We are *in* Christ, fully identified with him. We are no longer failures, worthless, or hopeless. No matter what label others have put on us, the only one that matters is the one put on us by Jesus.

This point comes home powerfully through this key verse, Galatians 2:20 (NIV): "I have been crucified with Christ and I no longer live, but Christ lives in me. The life I now live in the body, I live by faith in the Son of God, who loved me and gave himself for me." Thanks to Jesus, I have a new identity.

Living in the Great Exchange

The first truth we want to explore is that we have been "crucified with Christ." Jesus paid the price we couldn't pay to give us freedom from sin and eternal life. This was made possible, according to Romans 6:3: "When we were joined with Christ Jesus in baptism, we joined him in his death."

In verse 6, Paul then makes the point that "we know that our old sinful selves were crucified with Christ so that sin might lose its power in our lives."

As we learned in a previous chapter, "For you died to this

life, and your real life is hidden with Christ in God," (Col. 3:3). It is a powerful truth; when embraced, it puts a new perspective on how we live. Our actions are no longer about ourselves but about the One who lives inside us. Our actions are no longer about our personal rights because we died with Christ, and dead people have no rights. We are free from a performance-based relationship with the God we love. We are no longer identified or judged by all those labels. We are accepted and empowered by the God who loves us and gave his only Son for us.

There is a story I read many years ago that says it so well.

The Story of the Caterpillar Turned Butterfly

You know how a caterpillar becomes a butterfly through the process of metamorphosis. The caterpillar weaves a cocoon around itself but at just the right time, the caterpillar breaks out of the cocoon and emerges as a butterfly. If you were to see a butterfly, it would never occur to you to say, "Hey everybody! Come look at this good-looking converted worm!" Why not? It was a worm. And it was converted. No, now it is a new creature, and you don't think in terms of what it was. You see it as it is now: a butterfly.[3]

In the same way, God sees us as his new creation in Christ. We were like the caterpillar, weaving cocoons around

---

[3] Steve McVey. "The Butterfly Story. *Grace Walk*. (Eugene, OR: Harvest House, 1995).

ourselves—building walls to protect ourselves, hiding our sins so others wouldn't know the real us, or being enslaved by an addiction that seemed impossible to break. At the right time, however, we were freed from the cocoon by the power of our God. In God, we are his new creations in Christ. We are no longer trapped in the cocoons.

Although you might not always act like a good butterfly— you might land on things you shouldn't or forget you are a butterfly and crawl around with your old worm buddies or, I might add, still see yourself as a worm, which is a great obstacle to growing in Christ—you are never going to be a worm again! You are a beautiful butterfly with the potential of living in the freedom and victory of the Lord Jesus Christ. Let's look into this further.

The good news is that I was also raised to life with Christ when he rose from the dead. Paul makes the point in 1 Corinthians 1:30 that "God has united you with Christ."

In Galatians 2:20 we read, "But Christ lives in me." Wherever life is, death isn't! Profound! He who is life, resident in the believer, conquers death for that believer. We live in Christ by the power of the Holy Spirit. We enjoy the life Jesus won for us through his death and resurrection.

Ephesians 1:19–20 gives us the key to living life to its fullest when it reveals that the same power that raised Christ from the dead lives in us. That's a lot of power!

As believers, we live far beneath our inheritance in Christ Jesus. We have settled for the assumption, "I asked Jesus into my heart, and I am trying my best to live for him." God has so much more in store for us, so much more for us to experience—living in the power, victory, and authority of the name of Jesus. How could it be any different when Jesus lives in me? This brings us to a key to living this kind of life.

Looking again at Galatians 2:20, we see that we are now living by faith in the Son of God. We are no longer depending on our own ability, our own righteousness, our own behavior, or our works. Our hope, our dependency, and our faith are in the Lord, Jesus Christ.

All of what I have written to this point is truth supported by the Word of God. However, we will never experience it if we do not receive it by faith. In faith, I rely on him to live his life in and through me. In faith, I embrace his promises and provision.

Romans 3:22 makes it very clear that "we are made right with God by placing our faith in Jesus Christ." Or, as Romans 1:17 puts it, "The just shall live by faith." Everything God has for us or says about us is received by faith. Every day we are dependent upon our God for our very lives. We may not realize this and, unfortunately, try to bear our burdens and carry the responsibilities for ourselves and loved ones ourselves. But the truth is that Jesus is our burden bearer; he is the One who is in control.

In 1 Peter 5:7, Peter urges us to "cast all our cares on him, for he cares for us."

In Matthew 11:28 (NLT), Jesus invites us to "Come to me all of you who are weary and carry heavy burdens and I will give you rest."

In Hebrews 1:3, we are also encouraged to trust him with our lives and know that, as God, he has all under control.

A beautiful picture of Christ living in us and operating through us by faith is found in Ephesians 3:17: "Then Christ will make his home in your hearts as you trust in him. Your roots will grow down into God's love and keep you strong."

Incidentally, we may think we have to clean up our homes (our hearts) before we can have Jesus come into them and make his home with us; however, the opposite is true. Jesus comes into our homes and makes his home in us so that the process of cleansing can begin.

It is a matter of trust and faith in his Word and his promises and his sacrificial gift of himself for me. Just think—Jesus loved me enough to give himself up into death for me. I may love one of you dearly. However, I wouldn't sacrifice one of my children for you. What a sacrifice Father God made when he sent Jesus to earth for the sole purpose of dying a sinner's death on the cross for sinful mankind. He loved us that much. Jesus was willing to leave the glories of heaven, a place without sin, to come to the earth among sinful mankind, to be scorned and rejected by the very ones he had come to save, to die a horrendous death on the cross for all, even those who would reject his sacrifice—all because he was compelled by love.

Living in the Confidence of His Love

When Jesus said, "It is finished," he was declaring that he had been faithful to his mission and the redemption of mankind was completed. Confirmation is found in Romans 8:34: "for Christ Jesus died for us and was raised to life for us." Did you note the reason? It was for us! This is the greatest expression of love we will ever see.

The writer of Romans 8:38 declares, "I am convinced that nothing will ever be able to separate us from God's love." Are we convinced? When challenges or unexpected crises come into our lives, when storms threaten to pull us under, are we still convinced? When we fail notably and do something shameful, are we still convinced?

When we have questions about whether or not God loves us, all we have to do is look to the cross. This is the great message: He loves us so much that he sent Jesus; Jesus loves us so much that he came. Their sole purpose was to bring us into a relationship with him: to live out this life in victory and to experience his hand of blessing and his abundant grace and mercy; to close our eyes in this world and to awaken living in the glories of heaven forever.

To complete the picture that Galatians 2:20 paints for us, let's look at John 10:11. It presents Jesus as a good shepherd who "sacrifices his life for the sheep."

That phrase reminds us of Psalm 23, which reveals that the Lord, our shepherd, supplies all our needs and guards us with his very life. I would encourage you to personalize this psalm. It would sound like this: "The Lord is *my* shepherd; *I* have all that *I* need."

The One who gave his life for me is the One whom I can trust with my life. There is no place to go but to him for life, for wholeness, for healing, for protection. His life is in me; his life is for me. Life cannot get any better than this!

Thoughts to Ponder

1. What were some labels you gave yourself or others put on you while you were growing up? What effect did those labels have on you?

2. Why is it so much easier for people to believe those labels than the ones that scripture puts on them?

3. Why is it so much easier to believe lies about ourselves and stay in places of bondage than to walk in victory and freedom?

CHAPTER 7

Righteousness Enjoyed on
the Other Side of *But*

... And be found in him, not having a righteousness
of my own that comes from the law, but that which
is through faith in Christ—the righteousness that
comes from God on the basis of faith.

—Philippians 3:9 (NIV)

W hen we were little children, we had great fun dressing
up in our mothers' clothes or wearing ballerina or
princess costumes. We would live in the land of make-believe
and find joy in being someone different.

As we got older, we put away those dress-up games and
exchanged them for another form of the dress-up game. We
clothed ourselves with trappings of the world to disguise the

things that were within. We put up walls and barriers and assumed a false identity so that people couldn't see the real us. Pretending to be all put together and to be people whom our peers would respect fooled many of them and gave us respectability. But it couldn't fool us. We were filled with shame, regret, guilt, anxiety, and fear—anything but righteous. We were threatened by transparency or vulnerability, both out of the question because they brought the real possibility of rejection. We assumed that revealing ourselves would bring rejection. So we played dress-up. We did anything we could for self-preservation. Nothing changed the people we were on the inside or how we viewed ourselves. All the disguises only put us further into despair and hopelessness. The problem is that we tried to be righteous before we were *made* righteous.

But then came Jesus, inviting us to exchange our dress-up clothes for real ones, offering us a love that equaled acceptance, a release from guilt and condemnation, and a new garment of righteousness. This is the good news of living on the other side of *but*.

First, just know that you were not alone in playing dress-up as an adult. We've all been guilty of thinking we could be good enough, do enough, and pretend enough to make ourselves acceptable to ourselves and, most of all, to God. The Bible lets us know that it is impossible to exchange pretense for authenticity. Just think about actors and actresses who have become identified with roles they played in movies or TV series. Those persons may be what they are like in real life, away from the cameras, but they probably are not. They have been labeled on a basis other than reality. They are not who we think they are, wearing clothes that don't belong to them, ones they don't deserve and that don't clearly reveal who they are. I trust you are getting the picture.

Needing New Clothes

The Bible lets us know that all of us, when living without Christ, dress ourselves in clothes that may make us acceptable to others and may hide who we really are. However, we can't clothe ourselves with garments fit for our king. In Isaiah 64:6, we read that all our righteousness is as filthy rags. That's not very becoming; that's why we need a *but*.

There are at least two instances in the Old Testament that demonstrate the need for new clothes. The first one is found in the story of Joseph. He had been sold into slavery by his own brothers. While in Potiphar's home, he was falsely accused of trying to rape Potiphar's wife and was thrown into prison. Because God gave him the ability to interpret dreams, he was summoned by the pharaoh so that he might interpret two of his dreams. Before he could appear before the pharaoh, he was cleaned up and given new garments to wear.

The other illustration is found in the book and person of Esther. She was brought into the king's harem for the sole purpose of pleasing the king and replacing Vashti as the new queen. It took a year of preparation, with oils and perfumes, before the women were invited to spend a night with the king. When it was Esther's turn to come before the king, she yielded to the advice of Hegai, the eunuch in charge of the harem, and wore what he recommended.

When we are invited to come before the king of kings, there is a process of preparation. We are washed clean through the blood of Jesus (oils and perfume). Then we need to be clothed in garments worthy of him. This garment can't be bought; it is given. It is the garment of righteousness. Note that this garment does not just go over the old ones. We are stripped bare (the old man, the sins and shame of our pasts) and given this robe of righteousness, the garment needed for those who come into his presence.

Psalm 14:3 and Psalm 53:3 give us a true picture of mankind when they state that "no one does good, not a single one" because, as Romans 3:23 makes clear, "For everyone has sinned; we all fall short of God's glory."

As David lays it out in Psalm 51:5, we are completely void of original righteousness: "For I was born a sinner—yes, from the moment my mother conceived me." This sin is known as original sin. No matter how righteous we look to others, no matter how hard we try to clean up our acts, God sees us as we are. That's why there is a *but*. The reality of who God is for us, how he sees us, and what he has done for us is often clouded by what we have done or had done to us.

Let me give you an illustration. Let's say I am holding before you a twenty-dollar bill and ask you its value. You respond that it is worth twenty dollars. Now suppose I wad up the bill, stamp on it, and then show it to you, asking you its value. You would respond that it is still worth twenty dollars. No matter what we have experienced, the names or labels people gave us, the defeats, the bondages, and the damage that we have experienced, God sees that our value and worth are still the same. Only God can take that twenty-dollar bill (a human life) and remove all the wrinkles and damage, making it new again.

Discovering the Source of Righteousness

This is confirmed in Philippians 3:9 (NIV): "And being found in him, not having a righteousness of my own that comes from the law, but that which is through faith in Christ." However, before we linger on the precious *but* that exists because of Jesus, let's look at mankind's attempts to gain the righteousness they know is needed.

To begin, we look at the story of the rich, young ruler in Mark 10. He came to Jesus and asked what he needed to do to be saved. Jesus recited for him the commandments, leaving out the first three. The man declared that he had obeyed all these from his youth but realized there was still something missing. So Jesus told him to sell all he had, give it to the poor, and follow him. Does that mean that is what we need to do to be made right with God? Absolutely not! Jesus was approaching this young man from where he was. He wanted to do something for his salvation. The fact that he went away sad revealed what Jesus already knew: His first love was not God but riches. It was really a matter of his heart.

We are made right and righteous through faith in Jesus, not by our works—our own efforts to become righteous. Romans

3:20–28 and Romans 4:6 emphasize that point. When we try to be righteous in our own strength, in our own abilities, our own acts of righteousness, we are saying that we don't need Jesus. As it is written in Galatians 2:21, "For if keeping the law could make us right with God, then there was no need for Jesus to die."

The effort to earn God's forgiveness, his love, and his righteousness is a pit that many of us have fallen into when we have failed to live up to the standard of holiness found in Jesus. The very good news is that the same grace that brought us to him also keeps us in him. As in Romans 8:1, we are assured that "there is no condemnation for those who belong to Christ Jesus."

If we cannot clothe ourselves with righteousness or be good enough to earn righteousness, how do we become fit to come before the king? This is a question that everyone needs to answer correctly. It is a matter of life and death—forever.

In Titus 3:5, we read that "he saved us, not because of the righteous things we had done, but because of his mercy. He washed away our sins, giving us a new birth and new life through the Holy Spirit." This salvation becomes possible only by the blood of Jesus.

Romans 5:17 mentions righteousness as God's gift that can only be received through faith in Jesus.

Just ask yourself how many good deeds the thief on the cross did to receive the promise from Jesus, "Today you will be with me in paradise"? The answer, of course, is *none*. He believed, to his dying breath, that Jesus was who he said he was, and his faith saved him. His score is the same number of good deeds that any of us can claim for our salvation. We are redeemed through the righteousness of God. We read in Philippians 3:9, "I no longer count on my own righteousness through obeying the law; rather, I become righteous through faith in Christ." Salvation is a gift; righteousness is a gift.

If you want a *wow* moment, look at Isaiah 61:10: "I am overwhelmed with joy in the Lord my God! For he has dressed me with the clothing of salvation and draped me in a robe of righteousness." No person can be dressed any better than that!

Dressing Properly for Our King

The way I'm dressed should have an effect on how I live. If I am wearing an old pair of jeans and a T-shirt, it is appropriate dress for working around the house, cleaning, or pulling weeds out in the yard. But I am not appropriately dressed for an audience with the queen. For this occasion, I will wear my finest or splurge on something new and suitable for my audience with the queen. When we were wearing our own clothes of righteousness, filthy rags, the way we lived might have been appropriate for the world in which we were living. But now we are clothed in righteousness and are invited and empowered to live righteously. The text below states the beautiful reality.

> God has united you with Christ Jesus. For our benefit God made him to be wisdom itself. Christ made us right with God; he made us pure and holy, and he freed us from sin. (1 Corinthians 1:30)

The other side of *but* is that we no longer have to try to clothe ourselves in righteousness by what we do or don't do, but we are clothed in righteousness because of what Jesus did. Great exchange—our filthy rags for garments of righteousness earned for us by what Jesus did on the cross, given to us freely because of who he is. Now we are free to live in the righteousness he has provided and live righteously by the power of his life living within us. This would be an impossibility but for Jesus!

Thoughts to Ponder

1. Have you ever "played dress-up" as a believer? How do you exchange the dress-up act for the real thing?

2. How do you see yourself: as a wrinkled twenty-dollar bill or a new, crisp one? Why?

3. Describe what it means to you to wear the robe of righteousness.

CHAPTER 8

Kingdom Living Proclaimed on the Other Side of *But*

But you are not like that, for you are a chosen people. You are royal priests, a holy nation, God's very own possession. As a result, you can show others the goodness of God, for he called you out of the darkness into his wonderful light.

—1 Peter 2:9

In this country, we do not have a king or queen sitting on a throne and directing the affairs of the United States. So we may not understand fully what it would be like to be a member of a royal family. A king or queen has privileges and responsibilities that commoners lack. Sovereigns have authority over all who live in their nations. They manage and enjoy their nations' wealth. They receive love, honor, and respect from their people if they are worthy rulers, and the world takes notice. The clothes they wear and the confidence they exude are in accordance with the positions they hold. They know who they are and what they have. They are royalty.

Now imagine being born into that world. All that belongs to your parent belongs to you. You didn't do anything to gain the wealth, privileges, honor, and respect of the people in your land. You got it from your inheritance—being born into the royal family.

Through the scriptures we learn that we, as believers, indeed live in a kingdom. Our king is the God of the universe, creator of heaven and earth, upholding all things by the word of his power. When we sing songs to worship and praise his majesty, we acknowledge God as the king of all kings. To understand fully what is ours, we need to read the description of his kingdom as revealed in the following passages:

- Romans 14:17: It has righteousness, peace, and joy.
- Luke 10:19: It has the demonstration of power and authority.
- Luke 11:20: It is where he casts out demons.
- Matthew 8:16: It is where he heals the sick.

Being Born Into Royalty

When we were born again, we were born into the royal family with all its privileges and responsibilities. For those living as royalty in the kingdom of God, 1 Corinthians 4:20 lets us know that "the Kingdom of God is not just a lot of talk; it is living by God's power." The good news is that his kingdom is not hypothetical; it is not imaginary. We need to know who we are and what we have as royalty. Let's read Peter's description.

> But you are not like that, for you are a chosen people. You are royal priests, a holy nation, God's very own possession. As a result, you can show others the goodness of God, for he called you out of the darkness into his wonderful light. (1 Peter 2:9)

We should feel excited when we start to meditate on just what it means to be a part of God's kingdom, no longer living in darkness but in the wonderful light of his presence with all the rights and privileges that are ours in him.

In Matthew 6:33, we read that it is of utmost importance to seek the kingdom of God. The world seems to have so much to offer, so much that attracts us. When we see the emptiness of all that the world offers us, we are brought face to face with the reality of our need for a savior. We embrace Jesus as our Lord and Savior, and we are born again. We are now translated out of the kingdom of darkness and have become part of God's kingdom (Col. 1:13).

Just think—Luke 12:32 tells us that "it gives your Father great happiness to give you the Kingdom." This gift was part of his plan from all eternity. When Adam and Eve were created, they were to rule over the world he had created, as the story goes in Genesis 1:28. However, sin entered, and the devil took what was to be theirs. But God had a plan, and in Jesus, the plan could be realized: God's people would reside again with him in his kingdom, doing kingdom business.

But we will arrive there not by our own strength or ability, not by our own determination and will. "It is not by force nor by strength, but by my Spirit," as the prophet wrote in Zechariah 4:6. We are no match for the devil and the lawlessness he instigates, but the devil is no match for God. God is the one who holds all power and authority.

Living as Royalty

In the name of Jesus, we also have power and authority to see the devil defeated in our lives, in the lives of our loved ones, and in the chaotic world. That is the exciting truth. It is recorded in Matthew 28:18,19 that when Jesus was leaving the disciples to return to heaven, he told them, "I have been given all authority in heaven and on earth. Go therefore and make disciples of all nations, baptizing them in the name of the Father and the Son and the Holy Spirit."

The same authority Jesus has is given to his children who by faith take their rightful place in battle calling on the name of Jesus and operating by the power of the Holy Spirit. In Acts 1:8, this power was promised to the disciples and to us when Jesus said, "But you will receive power when the Holy Spirit comes upon you." When you said *yes* to Jesus, the Holy Spirit made himself resident in your life to empower you for a life of victory. That is one of the benefits of being in his kingdom, identified with and belonging to the king.

In Philippians 3:20, we read, "But we are citizens of heaven, where the Lord Jesus Christ lives." What exactly does that mean, and how then should we live?

First, it means that we are in the world, not of the world. The world where we live is just temporary. Heaven is our eternal home. In 1 Thessalonians 2:12, Paul admonishes the believers to "live your lives in a way that God would consider worthy. For he called you to share in his Kingdom and glory."

I submit to you that Paul meant more than that the believers should not do anything wrong. He was challenging them to live in the fullness of their inheritance in Christ. They were to realize who they were—the perks, as it were, of being the king's children. They were to live with the realization that they were children of God and act accordingly.

> There is a story told of a man who lived in a foreign land who desired with all his heart to come to America. So, he worked very hard and saved the money to come. He finally saved enough and made passage on a ship that was coming to America. When the journey came to an end and he was finally going to have his dream fulfilled, the captain of the ship said, "May I ask you a question? Did we somehow offend you? You never

came to the dining table although we had a place reserved for you."

The man responded, "Oh, I barely had enough money to purchase my ticket to come to America. I did not have any money for the food, so I stayed in my cabin and ate cheese and crackers."

The captain responded, "I am so sorry you did not understand that with the ticket came all the benefits. All the food was free and for your enjoyment."

What a hard way to learn a lesson. What does God need to do in our lives to help us understand all the benefits that come with our ticket to kingdom living?

Because this world is just temporary, we are to live as eternal beings with eternal perspectives and eternal destiny. We are told in Hebrews 12:28 that "since we are receiving a Kingdom that is unshakable, let us be thankful and please God by worshiping him with holy fear and "awe". It becomes a matter of perspective; the right perspective produces the right response.

Our faithfulness to our identity as kingdom kids brings the blessing described in 2 Peter 1:11: "Then God will give you a grand entrance into the eternal Kingdom of our Lord and Savior Jesus Christ." Our response should match that of a man who heard Jesus teach from the parable of the great feast. He exclaimed, "What a blessing it will be to attend a banquet in the kingdom of God."

Living for Eternity

It becomes clear that there are two aspects of kingdom living. There is the potential life we can live now as children of the king. This life manifests in and through our lives by the power of the Holy Spirit. We stand in his authority when doing what he has called us to do, living as he has called us to live. We are royalty because of the One who made us royal. We walk in our authority as children of the king, robed in righteousness, wearing the whole armor of God as described in Ephesians 6. We stand ready for battle, separated from the world and its demands, confident in our identity as children of the king. This is kingdom living in the present.

There is also kingdom life in the hereafter—life that goes on forever with the One who calls us his own. I remember an insight God gave me when we attended the graduation of our oldest son. The university was recognizing men and women with honorary degrees. It was really a big deal. God just spoke to my heart and said, "See how the world honors its own. That is nothing compared to how I honor mine."

This recollection leads me to another thought, something that we just saw in 2 Peter 1:1. Just think how it would feel to be welcomed into the presence of the Lord with great fanfare like a war hero when he comes home from the battle with medals. That welcome indicates a job well done and one that is rewarded accordingly.

To wrap up this chapter, I would like to compare our lives with and without God to the story of Cinderella. Cinderella was born into an affluent home, as were Adam and Eve in the garden of Eden. But when her mother died and her father remarried, she was reduced to the status of a servant (reduced to a slave of sin because of Adam and Eve's fall into temptation). Even as an invitation was issued to all the young women to come to the ball, God has given all of us an invitation to come to his banquet table. We tried to come dressed in our own garments of righteousness, but our disguises were exposed, and we fled. However, the prince (Jesus) came looking for us, found us, and restored to us what we had lost. We were no longer slaves. Actually we gained more than we had ever lost and became royalty. We are now fit to come to the banquet table and celebrate our inheritance forever. We are a part of a new kingdom in which, as is fitting in a fairy tale, we live happily ever after.

Only the good news is that this story is not a fairy tale; this is truth rooted in Jesus himself. He came to "seek and to save that which was lost"—you and me. He paid dearly for us to be a part of his family, to live in the kingdom of light, and to experience all the blessings this offers. The truth is that our life is not our own anymore; we have been bought with a price. "We are God's very own possession ... called out of the darkness into his wonderful light." (Col. 1:13) This is called kingdom living on the other side of *but*.

Thoughts to Ponder

1. When you pray the Lord's Prayer and say, "Thy Kingdom come," what are you asking the Lord to do?

2. How would you describe kingdom living? How does that understanding impact the way you live?

3. What is your Cinderella story?

CHAPTER 9

New Destiny Is Promised on the Other Side of *But*

But now you are free from the power of sin and
have become slaves of God. Now you do those
things that lead to holiness and result in eternal
life.

—Romans 6:22

L et's pretend you have just received a special offer. All you
need to do is fill out a card and mail it in, and you will be
eligible for a drawing. If you win, you will be given a free ten-
day cruise to your dream vacation destination. Several months
later, you receive notice that you have won the grand prize. The
trip is yours. The excitement and anticipation of your destiny
are more than you can contain. You tell everyone you know that

you are going on your dream vacation with all expenses paid. Wow! Can it get any better than that?

The answer is yes. You see, we have won the trip of a lifetime: eternity in heaven. All expenses have been paid by the blood of Jesus. We have met all the requirements: our lives given to Jesus, our sins forgiven, clothed in his garment of righteousness. The day is coming when we will be able to cash in our prize and take the final trip of a lifetime—to heaven, with our Savior who made it all possible.

I had always dreamed of going to Hawaii; but with eight children and all the financial challenges we had over the years, the dream seemed just that, a dream. Then something happened. On our fortieth wedding anniversary, our children surprised us with a trip to Hawaii, all expenses paid: airplane tickets, hotel rooms, and spending money to enjoy activities and beautiful sights available to tourists. Imagine our surprise and our pleasure at such a gift. That trip was everything I had imagined it would be—and more.

My husband dreamed of going to Alaska. I am partial to warm climates, so this was not exactly a place I would have chosen. However, the cold is not a negative for my husband. I thought it only fair that if I could have my dream come true, he should be able to experience his dream as well. All our children, of course, were adults and on their own; the financial challenges that would have prevented the trip were past, so it was within the realm of possibility. For our fiftieth anniversary, we booked a cruise bound for Alaska, and off we went. This was an awesome experience of drinking in so many of God's marvelous works.

In God's great love and awesome provision, we even had great weather.

However, God has given us an even greater dream and a greater destination. We ended the last chapter discussing the eternal kingdom that is ours in Christ, our final destination. The dream that we, as believers, have of seeing our blessed Savior face to face and living with him forever can be fulfilled if we make the right choice and meet the conditions—all made possible through Jesus, his death, his resurrection, and the power of the Holy Spirit. Because of his mercy in not giving us what we deserve and his grace in giving us what we don't deserve, we can come into the relationship with Jesus that secures our eternal destiny. We want to look at this from three vantage points: our choice, the condition, and the promises to reach our new destiny on the other side of *but*.

Making the Right Choice God's Way

It is a choice; he invites. He doesn't coerce us, but he does create the hunger to experience what he offers and enables us to respond to his invitation to come. In his own words in John 4:14, Jesus offers the woman at the well (and all sinners) the chance to drink of the living water, Jesus himself, and never be thirsty again. He offers himself; we respond and come. We hear this response in a famous song.

> Just as I am without one plea,
> but that Thy blood was shed for me

And that Thou bidst me come to Thee
Oh, Lamb of God, I come, I come.

This is the most important decision we will ever make to find the destiny we have always craved. Let me add here: When we are going to take that trip of a lifetime, there is a certain amount of preparation that we need to make. We have to clear our calendars (unclutter our lives), make sure we have a valid passport (the blood of Jesus), and pack our bags (righteousness, peace, and forgiveness, to name a few). The trip is free, but it still costs us something—giving the control over to the ship's captain and letting him set the agenda for the sights to be seen. We surrender our lives to the Lord and let him set the agenda for our lives.

It is exciting to realize that this decision offers the adventure of our lives—dreams and victories we might have postponed, as with my trip to Hawaii. But God has better plans for us, greater adventures in living. The ultimate choice, with the ultimate reward, is presented by scripture.

As it is written in Galatians 6:8, "Those who live only to satisfy their own sinful nature will harvest decay and death from that sinful nature. But those who live to please the Spirit will harvest everlasting life from the Spirit."

This is made possible according to Romans 6:22: "But now you are free from the power of sin and have become slaves of God. Now you do those things that lead to holiness and result in eternal life."

As Galatians 5:1 declares, "It is for freedom that Christ has set you free."

We choose; he empowers the choices; the choices equal a new life and new destiny.

We take a stand like Joshua, who declared, "Choose this day who you will follow ... but as for me and my family we will serve the Lord," in Joshua 24:15.

As we can see, this choice is not automatic but conditional. Not only is there a *but*; there is also an *if*. We see this pairing many times in scripture. Here are a few examples.

> If any man be in Christ, he is a new creation. (2 Corinthians 5:17)

> If we confess our sins, he is faithful and just to forgive and cleanse. (1 John 1:9)

> If you refuse to take up your cross and follow me you are not worthy of being mine. (John 10:18)

> If you cling to your life, you will lose it, but if you give up your life for me you will find it. (John 10:19)

Throughout scripture, it is clear that there is an eternal destiny awaiting those who meet the condition—the big *if*.

The *if* for salvation, for our eternal destiny in heaven with our Savior forever, is belief. We find it specified in passages like John 3:15: "so that everyone who believes in him will have eternal life." This is repeated many times in scripture. In John 6:40–46, we read that all who see his son and believe in him should have eternal life.

What a relief! I don't have to be good enough. I don't have to do enough. I simply have to believe and to embrace Jesus as my Lord and Savior. I am now able to take the steps to holiness, not to receive salvation and my eternal destiny—but because I have received salvation and with it the desire and empowerment to live a holy life that is pleasing to God.

I realize that we have shared some of these truths in other chapters, but they are too good not to repeat. When we received the trip to Hawaii from our children, all we had to do was accept and enjoy it. We didn't have to do anything to earn it. God has provided a way for us to take the trip of a lifetime. We are destined for heaven! It is made possible by faith, by becoming one with him through Jesus Christ.

People are so often focused on this world that an eternal destiny is the farthest thing from their thoughts. This I know, though—unless Jesus returns when we are still alive, all of us will die. Billy Graham once commented that if we heard on the news that he had died, it wasn't true; that news would mean that he had really just begun to live. This is the hope of the believer.

Holding onto God's Promises

Finally, we want to look at the promises. Jesus told his disciples and told us that he was going home to his Father before us, that he would be preparing a place for us, and that he would come for us. As written in John 14:1–4, the motivation for this preparation was that we would be with him forever, living out our eternal destiny in our eternal resting place in the presence of our precious Savior. Peter elaborates on this inheritance and this eternal destiny.

> And we have a priceless inheritance—an inheritance that is kept in heaven for you, pure and undefiled, beyond the reach of change and decay. And through your faith, God is protecting you by his power until you receive this salvation, which is ready to be revealed on the last day for all to see. (1 Peter 1:4–5)

Our eternal inheritance is secure in Jesus. To cement this even further, look at 2 Corinthians 5:1.

> For we know that when this earthly tent we live in is taken down (that is, when we die and leave this earthly body), we will have a house in heaven, an eternal body made for us by God himself and not by human hands. (2 Corinthians 5:1)

God has a plan that goes into eternity for each of our lives. We may be earthbound in our thinking, focusing on the present, but God is focused on heaven as he works in our lives. His ultimate desire and goal for each of us is that we spend eternity in heaven with him. His desire is for all to be saved and come to the knowledge of the truth, as written in 1 Timothy 2:4.

That's why he has revealed himself to us through his Son, Jesus, through his Word, and through daily provisions and wonders that surround us.

As I was cuddled up with God in prayer (just as my precious little dog was cuddled up with me), I reflected that there might be a million people pouring out their hearts before the Lord. Some might pray in praise and worship, some in great anguish of the soul, but we all would have the ear of God, knowing that he was listening and working in our lives, the lives of our families, and the affairs of the world, and all at the same time! That is the God we love and serve, the God who loves us outrageously and is drawing us ever closer so that we might experience the fullness and blessings of our eternal destiny.

Speaking of our eternal destiny, when my heart's desire was to go to Hawaii, I thought I knew what to expect. I imagined what Hawaii would look like, the experiences I would have, and the joy and pleasure of finally realizing my dream. I am here to tell you that my experience was even better than I ever could have imagined.

When we were preparing for our trip to Alaska, we heard about the wonderful sights we would see and the great experiences we would have as we toured Alaska. Again, our experience was more than we had imagined.

Before both these trips, we thought we knew what was in store and anticipated what we would experience when we reached our destination. But words cannot fully describe what a person can experience. We saw majestic mountains, beautiful clear waters, glaciers falling into the ocean, and the sun seemingly falling into the ocean as it set. We experienced different cultures and scenery. We had no idea what an impact these trips would have on us. Words cannot begin to describe adequately all the blessings we experienced on these trips.

I trust you are seeing the parallel. I know how I have imagined heaven. I have read the Word and what it tells me about heaven. I have heard the accounts of many who said they died and went to heaven. But I am confident that when I get there, it will be beyond what I ever could have imagined. That, my friends, is your new destiny on the other side of *but*—prepared just for you. It can't get any better than that!

Thoughts to Ponder

1. Which statement do you agree with and why? "He is so focused on heaven that he is no earthly good," or "The more focused on heaven he is, the more earthly good he will be."

2. Which dream of yours became a reality, and how did God reveal himself to you through it?

3. How do we make preparation for the trip of a lifetime— our eternal destiny?

CHAPTER 10

Blessings We've Received on the Other Side of *But*

All praise to God, the Father of our Lord Jesus
Christ, who has blessed us with every spiritual
blessing in heavenly realms because we are united
with Christ.

—Ephesians 1:3

W hen our children were growing up, we were often
financially challenged. My husband was a good
provider, but we experienced those financial challenges because
of the decisions we made, as a family, to follow Jesus. My husband
was a pastor in a mainstream denomination, and he got saved
and challenged his congregation to do the same. The proverbial
straw that broke the camel's back was the service when he had

an altar call for those wanting to give their hearts to the Lord. Due to the circumstances surrounding this event, he was gently squeezed out of the church. The years that followed were rich with God's presence even in the midst of many challenges and much adversity, too many instances to share in this chapter. These events do set the stage, though, for what I am about to share.

Christmas in our home was an exciting time because of all the music, the decorations, and, of course, the gifts. We were financially challenged and didn't have the money to lavish gifts on our children. The good news is God's resources are unlimited. In his mercy and grace, he made every Christmas special. After reading the Christmas story in Luke 2, the children took turns opening their gifts, much to their joy and delight. God had blessed us out of his abundance, once again, in ways that only he could have imagined. He is a good God and does all things well.

Living in Freedom

We are ending this journey of investigating what it looks like to live on the other side of *but*, beginning appropriately with Paul in Ephesians 1:3. Paul bursts out in praise to God: "All praise to God, the Father of our Lord Jesus Christ, who has blessed us with every spiritual blessing in the heavenly realms because we are united with Christ." Did you notice the word *every*? In Christ Jesus, we lack nothing.

The psalmist expressed this exuberant praise, as well, in Psalm 103:2: "Let all that I am praise the Lord, may I never forget the good things he does for me." He continued by listing some of those divine gifts: forgiveness of sin, healing of diseases, redemption from death, crowning with love and tender mercies, and filling believers' lives with good things. If all God ever did for us was to give us life through his Son, redeem us from our sins, and give us passage into heaven, we would be the most blessed of people. However, as the psalmist wrote, and as we will discuss in many verses found in the scriptures, those gifts aren't all he has given us. There are so many blessings on the other side of *but*.

Before we look at some of those blessings revealed in scripture, I want to share a dream I had years ago. I was walking with a group of people on a road. Out in the distance were the bright lights of a city. As we drew closer, many people were on the other side of the road. They were returning to where we had been. I couldn't figure out why they wouldn't keep going to that beautiful city. Then I saw the obstacle to our destination. It was a deep, dark pit we had to go through to get to the city. I cried out to God to help me and took the first step down into the pit. Then I woke up. The bright city symbolized all the blessings God has for his children. God's requirement is that we surrender to him to receive them.

Now let's look at some of these blessings that we can experience on the other side of *but*.

According to 2 Timothy 1:7 we are told "God has not given us a spirit of fear and timidity, but of power, love, and self-discipline." It is God's gift to free us from fear and intimidation, to enable us to be bold in our walk with him and in the power he has provided to overcome challenges. The walls we have built for our self-protection are no longer necessary because we have discovered that he is our protector. We are now walking free of fear.

It takes the revelation by the Holy Spirit to recognize those walls. I remember going to a pastors' conference where the speaker said that there were wives who needed to forgive members of their congregations who had hurt their husbands and their ministries. I started crying but couldn't understand why. I had forgiven those who had hurt my husband, but God showed me that I had built up a wall of protection. My wall said, "Although I have forgiven you, I will keep you at a distance so that you can never hurt us again." This stance was a wall of protection from hurt. When the light of this place of darkness was revealed, the walls came down, and the darkness was dispelled. I know this is true because on our return home, members of the church saw a difference in me and how I related to them. Now I notice when I begin to construct a wall and before the wall is fully built, I ask God what about that person or that situation makes me feel like I need to protect myself? With revelation comes victory.

We have received the ability to love others and walk circumspectly, which is fitting for a child of God. We don't have to work up courage; it's ours by the power of God—a blessing on the other side of *but*.

> So you have not received a spirit that makes you
> fearful slaves. Instead, you received God's Spirit

when he adopted you as his own children. Now
we call him, "Abba, Father." (Romans 8:15)

A slave had no rights; however, the master dealt with the
slave was his choice, and the master was not answerable to
anyone. He might be cruel and demanding. He would generally
be unengaged and distant, not concerned with the needs or
concerns of his slave. What he said was law, and what he
demanded was fulfilled. That is what we experienced when we
were slaves to sin and ruled by the "ruler of this world."

We don't need to be fearful slaves, however—by God's
Spirit, we have been adopted by God, our Father, and are his
own children. We can come into God's presence, knowing
that we are loved and accepted. He loves us; he is never a cruel
taskmaster. We no longer live in fear as slaves but in freedom
and relationship as his children—a blessing on the other side
of *but*.

Living in the Promises of God

There is a precious verse, Psalm 73:26: "My flesh and my heart
may fail, but God is the strength of my heart and my portion
forever." I don't have to live on the side of defeat and failure
because God is alive in me. He has become my strength. The
power and possibility of victorious living are found in Jesus
through the Holy Spirit. A life of freedom can be found on the
other side of *but*.

We are encouraged in our faith—"because of his glory and
excellence, he has given us great and precious promises. These

are the promises that enable you to share his divine nature and escape the world's corruption caused by human desires," found in 2 Peter 1:4. These promises are made possible by the *buts* we have studied in this book. We'll look at a few.

When God made his covenants with Noah, with Abraham, with Moses, and with the believer in Christ, he based those covenants on his own nature as a covenant-keeping God. Throughout the Bible we find God being faithful to his people and to his Word. We read that "all God's promises are 'yes'." (2 Corinthians 1:20). There is a saying: "If God said it, I believe it, and that settles it." That covers all God's promises. That means everything we need has been given to us to live on the other side of *but*.

Many of you who are reading this book have experienced the breaking of promises.

- A spouse who had said, "I will love you until death parts us," one day came to you and said, "I don't love you anymore; I want a divorce."
- A friend said, "You are my best friend forever," but a challenge came into the relationship, and the friend walked away and never made contact with you again.
- Our culture has made many promises that have turned out to be false. This medicine will cure you; this drug will make the pain go away; this house, this car, or this job will bring you happiness and make you feel fulfilled. Sometimes just the opposite happened. You remained

sick, you became addicted to the drug, or you "got it all" and were miserable.

God's promises are not like that. They are *yes* because they are backed up by God himself. He has said of himself, "I am the Lord, I change not." Hebrews 8:6 informs us that we have a better covenant, based on better promises, through Jesus. The One who is holy, the One who never lies, the One who is the Alpha and Omega and all the in-betweens of our lives is the One who has made the promises. We know him, so we also know we can trust him to keep his word.

The question for the day, then, is, "Why aren't we living in the confidence of all the promises and blessings? Why are we still living on the wrong side of *but* in so many areas of our lives?" I believe that it is because we have grown used to living there. The devil, the world, and our flesh all try to deny the possibility of a life without fear or defeat. We taste the good gifts of God but lose sight of them in the midst of the storms and challenges of life. It doesn't have to be that way, and maybe, until you read this book, you never saw there was another side.

Suppose God brought us to the place of salvation and then said, "Okay, now you are on your own. Show me what you have." What kind of God would he be then? He knows the answer, and so do we, really—without him, we have nothing and can do nothing. This is confirmed to us in the Gospel of John: "Without him you can do nothing." Maybe we don't find ourselves on the right side of *but* as much as we had hoped because we have relied on ourselves to get there—that is, if we even knew there was a right side of *but*. This is the secret: "I can do all things through Christ who strengthens me," as written in Philippians 4:13. Note the condition, "through Christ."

> So don't be misled, my dear brothers and sisters. Whatever is good and perfect is a gift coming down to us from God our Father, who created all the lights in the heavens. He never changes or casts a shifting shadow. (James 1:16–17 NIV)

In other words, we can trust the One who created us and has called us to be his own. He is for us and for our good because he is good and his ways are just and true. What a joy to know that there is the other side of *but*, and there we can experience all the blessings and goodness God has prepared for us.

Thoughts to Ponder

1. We have examined different aspects of living on the other side of *but*. Which one has impacted your life the most and why?

2. In this chapter we shared blessings we have received on the other side of *but*. Can you think of others that have touched your life?

3. What is your greatest challenge as a believer? What is your greatest victory as a believer?

Final Word to All My Readers

We have been on a journey throughout this book to discover just how God intended us to live our lives in the fullness of what he had planned and purposed. Although we have only scratched the surface of all that living on the other side of *but* promises, I pray that you will embrace what has been revealed through these pages and treasure what you have because of Jesus.

May you ever hold onto these truths: God loves you unconditionally, and he is *for* you. Focusing on these truths will enable you to live in the freedom and fullness of all God has for you on the other side of *but.*

I pray that as you continue to search the Scriptures, you will experience the joy and blessings of living in God's presence, on the other side of "but."

Printed in the United States
By Bookmasters